Minimalism

Explore The Immensely Efficient Methods Via Which You Can Incorporate New Habits, Streamline Your Living Space And Mental State, And Shift Towards A Minimalist Lifestyle By Embracing The Principle Of Simplicity

IdalinaDomingos

TABLE OF CONTNET

Comprehending The Mindset of Minimalism............. 1

Your brain is affected by clutter. 14

Describe minimalism..31

Assess the individuals that received a greater amount of your attention..43

Working with Minimalism 61

Living Simply in a Materialistic World........................75

Creating A Minimalist Mentality....................................87

The Five Aspects Of Smallness 103

Handling Money 129

Comprehending The Mindset of Minimalism

Minimalism aims to reduce the amount of worldly stuff you own by removing items from your home, especially those you don't need. This undoubtedly has some validity, but moderation is far more important.

The lesser-known aspect of moderation is that it just involves giving everything that matters to you more room in your life, heart, and mind. Being moderate doesn't mean trying to get rid of stuff. Moderation is about eliminating unnecessary things and surrounding yourself with what matters most.

Essentially, minimalism is a way of living that demands you to focus on whatever you deem important and noteworthy. It doesn't demand you give up certain cravings or lead a particular lifestyle. Profoundly, moderation simply asks you to become aware of your own needs. Rather than observing cultural norms, cliché culture, and consumerism, this attunement enables you to recognize what your heart yearns for and pursue.

A balanced perspective helps you know who you are and what you need. Whenever you practice mindfulness, you become aware of who you are, what you're capable of, and what you want out of life.

The moderate attitude also demonstrates the norms of letting go of everything that contradicts your values, beliefs, and standards, and replacing it with everything you know adds significance to your life.

Minimalism is more than just reducing the number of items and materialistic possessions; it also involves eliminating unlucky, pointless, and unhappy people, beliefs, ideas, activities, and standards from your life. If owning an iPhone makes your life better than owning two crappy phones, then you should purchase the iPhone; if staying out of a certain relationship makes you feel liberated and energized, then you should end it.

Being minimalist doesn't mean eschewing expensive or luxurious items in favor of a frugal lifestyle. Whatever you want to define, it is more about holding onto the things in your life that make it better than everything that detracts from its value.

Some minimalists believe that traveling is the epitome of a purpose-driven life. For this reason, they leave their two sacks behind and go to remote parts of the world, one place at a time, searching for the chance that comes with nightfall.

However, other minimalists believe owning a home is more important than anything else, so they prioritize building their own house or making adjustments that would allow them to pay off their mortgage faster rather than traveling.

As it turns out, moderation is crucial in helping you identify and prioritize your true needs. One of the main tenets of minimalism is paying attention to your needs.

Frequently, we believe we need something, but when it comes down to it, we want something very different that deviates from what we believe we need. For instance, you might believe you want to buy a car, but in the end, you only need some downtime and peace of mind from working sixteen hours a day.

It may be the most challenging aspect of the job. Because everything is something you brought into your life and house, getting rid of it isn't that difficult. Preparing yourself to deal with the idea of leaving them behind is the hardest part. To that purpose, you ought to cultivate a balanced perspective.

This wouldn't lessen the disarray. Those things will come out once more and create a comparable mess. Furthermore, your perspective would remain unchanged.

The important thing is to cultivate an approach that helps you recognize the value or importance of things in your daily life. You can eliminate everything that isn't on this list and concentrate on what matters. Moderation is the term for this simple interaction. There is no way to measure moderation. The degree to which you must reduce will depend on the type of person you are. However, if you try to practice moderation to better organize your home, you are on the wrong end of the spectrum.

It is incorrect to think of minimalism as a corrective cleaning technique. It is the final revision of the whole way of thinking.

The core of minimalism is realizing what is unnecessary and gradually getting rid of it. It would result in a clean environment, making you more productive and composed.

You should approach things methodically if you want to adopt the moderate route.

Recognize Your Motives

In this world, nothing happens without a reason. Until an outside force is introduced, things will frequently remain in their current state. Most objects in daily life fall under this fundamental material science principle. Assuming you are considering a moderate methodology, you should have some justification. Your decision will become more fragile if the explanations don't show or are unclear. For the technique to advance, it is imperative that the "why" be noted in this context.

List your motivations for adopting a moderate approach and write them down somewhere. It could very well be whatever woke you up. Maybe you're sick and weary of your house being disorganized. It usually stems from not noticing anything in your house that could inspire you. Perhaps you must simplify things because the steady choice weakness consumes much of your time.

There are many possible explanations, and each would strengthen your goal. But, if you don't have them clear, you'll eventually get complacent, and the chaos will return. You ought to articulate why you desire to live a simpler life. These will inspire you indefinitely.

Identifying the appropriate rationale for downsizing your house helps you look at things differently. Even if you have a good reason, many items that don't meet all the requirements will remain assets that you will find difficult to eliminate because they look messy or could potentially cause harm.

Connecting the Dots: The Effects of Clutter on Your Health, Peace, and Mind

I speak with numerous personal health and wellness specialists, so I have access to some insider knowledge. I never considered the possibility that the disorder in my house and personal life was the source of the confusion in my life—to say that it was cluttered would be an understatement—before my interest in self-awareness and inner calm reached its zenith. Please understand that I am not a klutz. I never leave anything behind. But back then, I could search for a specific item for several minutes, if not hours. This may not always indicate disorganization, but in my instance, it did.

Science demonstrates that hoarders, by nature, are mankind. Gathering and storing things is in our nature. While some of these objects hold sentimental significance, others are valuable in and of themselves. Whatever the rationale for preserving a forty-year-old coin present to you as a teenager, it is crucial to note that storing several sentimental items can lead to disarray and chaos. To some sense, clutter—which frequently occurs accidentally—is an outward manifestation of your feelings. What effect does this have on your well-being? It implies that, despite the emotion attached to that drawer full of' sentimental' objects, the drawer may have various effects on your life.

I apologize for the ambiguity in this sentence. Intentional or unintentional clutter impacts many aspects of your life. More precisely, clutter creates a barrier that prevents you from achieving inner serenity and well-being. There's still room for imagination with this. I have a question for you to answer to make things clear. How does it feel to rummage through a pile of garments to find your other shoe or rummage through a mound of stuff in the drawer to find your keys? People are sensitive to the surroundings in which they live. This implies that you might undoubtedly spend the rest of the day dissatisfied if you wake up in the morning scowling because you can't locate your other shoe or have to move a thousand things before you discover the one item you need for work. I hope this makes the confusion obvious. You can be frowning in displeasure or simply nodding your head in agreement. This is not a fabrication. Biology has demonstrated that human bodies are energy. Energy attracts energy, as you can recall from your rudimentary physics lessons. Since clutter is bad energy, if you have to sift through it all to get what you need first thing in the morning—or at any other time, for that matter—you are attracting bad energy into your life. Not only that, but clutter also has an impact on your life in several other ways, including:

Your brain is affected by clutter.

You probably had no idea that mental clutter has an impact on you! Few individuals are aware of the mental effects that clutter can have. Clutter, as I have said before, is an expression of negativity. Frustration arises when you dig through a mountain of other items to find an item you need for a project at work or home. Humans are naturally hoarders, as we have already shown. We are naturally inclined to gather things. Occasionally, we purchase items because we believe we will need them in the future. This is true even though you have only used it once since purchasing it two years ago, and that was immediately after you made the purchase. According to Yale researchers, the fear of parting with this thing hurts the two areas of your brain linked to pain. These spaces come to life anytime you consider parting with a "treasured" item, much like a brand-new neon sign. You'll see that the word "treasured" is enclosed in quotation marks. This is on purpose. This is the cause. Most of the items we consider significant or valuable but do not use often are not treasured. They are in disarray. This part of hoarding extraneous objects is an expression of emotional attachment.

Your brain's capacity to concentrate and process information is impacted by clutter. This has been demonstrated by science (a Princeton University research). According to the study, a physically busy workplace makes it harder to focus on the task and your brain. Performance suffers as a consequence, and stress levels rise.

Clutter makes your house and office messy.

This one should go without saying. Your life is messy if the clutter accumulates to oppressive proportions. Despite what the general public believes, clutter extends beyond its appearance. Allow me to pose a query to you. Why, in your opinion, do various email types have distinct folders in your email client? This is merely because clutter results from allowing items to gather in one location. An even more poignant illustration would be the misery of clearing out a +1000-email inbox. You invite viruses and rodents into your life when you allow clutter to become a part.

Clutter eliminates time.

How many minutes do you spend every morning trying to find the ideal shirt to match your suit, other shoes, or dress? Now consider this. How much time would you spend on your daily routine if you organized the things for your morning ritual methodically? I'd guess significantly less than you do now. How would you spend the extra time? I've discovered that when I tidy up and declutter my life and house, I have more time to carry out my rituals in a luxurious manner. I can avoid rushing through the morning traffic to work by maintaining organization. Because I use the time I would have spent looking for things in traffic to listen to relaxing music that promotes calm and tranquility for the day, I also don't become irritated when traffic to work moves slowly. Using just one trick, I can prioritize what has little to no substance in my life versus what matters. Furthermore, I've discovered that organizing things takes longer than "storing" them. Thus, by spending time organizing items rather than "storing" them, you enhance your welfare and establish balance in your life, in addition to sparing yourself from a possible headache.

THE BENEFITS OF BEING A MINIMALIST, CHAPTER 3.

1. GETTING REVIEWED:

It is not well acknowledged in society at the moment.

There is still a lot of skepticism regarding minimalism, especially in more conservative locations where social standing is still determined by the number of material items one can afford, even though tolerance for alternative lifestyles is growing gradually but steadily.

Therefore, minimalism could make it harder for you to be accepted as a contributing member of society, depending on the setting.

2. SOCIAL ISOLATION: Living a minimalist lifestyle may prevent you from attending social gatherings with your friends, leading to social isolation.

You might be unable to go on costly trips with your buddies because of your frugal lifestyle.

Adopting a minimalist lifestyle could lead to social isolation if your circle of friends is overly dependent on these showy activities.

3. REQUIRES A STRONG PERSONALITY: Minimalism and personality development are often closely related.

To avoid giving in to the need to purchase all the amazing things requires a strong sense of character.

Therefore, only if you possess this incredible inner strength will you be able to implement minimalism.

On the other hand, upholding this mindset can be extremely taxing, and many people could find it difficult to stick to minimalism over time.

4. FEAR OF LOSS OF CONVENIENCES: Acquiring a range of products can help with several issues and sometimes ease life's burdens.

People might, therefore, be reluctant to alter their consumption patterns out of fear that their quality of life will decline.

This fear may prevent many people from attempting minimalism, which is sad because many may gain by making less and leading a more modest lifestyle.

It can be difficult to go from materialism to minimalism.

Our material comforts rapidly grow ingrained in us, and altering our way of life can be challenging.

Taking small, daily steps towards simplicity instead of attempting major lifestyle adjustments may be more successful.

6. THE CONCEPT OF MINIMALISM IS ILLUMINATED:

It's common for critics of minimalism to claim that the term has no precise definition.

It is so challenging to defend leading this lifestyle without a definition.

Because of this, some people could be reluctant to engage in minimalism since they do not fully get it.

Chapter 2: The 'isms' of capitalism, consumerism, and other systems

Money

Under a capitalist political and economic system, private individuals control the nation's trade and industry to make a profit, as opposed to the state. For capitalism to function, markets must exist.

Marketplaces serve as venues for the exchange of commodities and services. These days, the methods used to accomplish this can be highly advanced, intricate, and complex. But if given the chance, markets will always develop on their own. Even the most archaic of societies exhibits them. As natural as the sun, rain, and air are markets.

Since just a small number of individuals often hold the means of production, and since these people frequently act in a greedy, repressive, and shortsighted manner, many people view capitalism with animosity. This has given rise to communism, the nasty antithesis of capitalism.

Shoplifting

Minimalism is opposed to consumerism. The preceding chapter provided a definition and description of minimalism. According to the economic theory of consumerism, the public benefits from ever-increasing consumption levels. Although capitalism makes consumerism feasible, it is not the only type of capitalism that may exist. There are other variations of capitalism.

Before the 19th century, when the phenomenon of mass manufacturing made it possible to produce ever-increasing quantities of material items, consumerism was not feasible. In Western countries, luxury and comfort were no longer exclusive to the ruling elites; they were now accessible to most people. People demanded more and more, never satisfied with enough.

When businesses in the industry realized they would soon go out of business if they continued to produce long-lasting products, the abhorrent phenomena of deliberate obsolescence started. This industrial strategy involved intentionally designing things to malfunction or break down after a predetermined time. Perceived obsolescence is an equally concerning phenomenon. It refers to the production of new versions of perfectly good things, and an enthusiastic advertising industry is tasked with convincing the public that they need the newer version of a product they currently own. There is great waste because of these two types of needless obsolescence.

Marxism

The weird and wicked ideology of communism was engulfing countless millions of people at the same time that Western nations like the USA, Britain, and Germany were industrializing. As a result, after the two world wars, half of the world turned communist. A few prominent communists thought that carnage was necessary to bring about a socialist paradise. These horrible concepts were put into practice with mass executions, concentration camps, and widespread hunger in nations like China, Cambodia, and Russia.

Aside from the fact that communism caused the deaths of many millions of people, its most significant flaw was that it was an ineffective system. Anyone who traveled to places like China, East Germany, or Russia in the 1970s will recall the extreme poverty there and the unusual and needless shortages of goods that Westerners take for granted. The 1980s saw the end of communism. It simply fell apart. It was ineffective everywhere. It was a sham. It was unable to satisfy or meet human desires. The Beatles and blue jeans were a match for the class struggle and material shortages of communism.

Market economies replaced communism in almost all of the former communist nations. Certain nations, like China, continued to be ruled by communists even after transitioning to capitalism.

The order had to be maintained, and communists were excellent at maintaining order even though they were completely incapable of doing anything else.

The Chinese developed a steadfast determination to match the Western quality of living. To accomplish this, they used a far larger scale version of what Germany and Japan had done following World War II. They deluged the globe with an oversupply of low-quality merchandise. The cost of numerous items, including electronics and apparel, dropped significantly. A massive boost was given to consumerism, which had grown nicely up until then. Suddenly, there were far more inexpensive things available everywhere in the world.

What the Chinese were doing was also adopted by other nations. Some formerly economically dormant regions and countries that burst into life economically were Southeast Asia, Russia, East Europe, Indonesia, and India.

Credit became more accessible during this time, and a global spending binge started, especially in the USA. It wasn't until the stock market meltdown in 2007 and 2008 that it slowed down significantly. People started to wonder if this method of doing things should continue worldwide. There was a broad backlash against consumerism, which had always existed. This response includes minimalism, which is viewed as a means of repairing consumerism's harm to the environment and human health.

Describe minimalism.

There is no set of rules or definitions for what constitutes moderation. Similar to uncomplicated living, moderation is a concept that has different meanings for different people. You must have a realistic understanding of moderation to learn more about it.

What is the minimalist movement?

"Moderation is essentially the ideal measure of something, not an absence of something," argues well-known moderate Nicholas Burroughs.

Being minimalist goes beyond material possessions. Being moderate means not wasting time, effort, or money on frivolous details but rather emphasizing and delivering on the necessities. As distinguished moderate Joshua Becker explained, "Moderation is the intentional advancement of the things we esteem most and disposing of the rest that diverts us from it."

For most of us, the preceding definition clarifies and rearranges moderation. A realistic idea of what you value most in daily life relates to moderation. Concentrate on the things that demand most of your attention, time, effort, and space, and then consciously get rid of everything else that stands in the way of your prized possessions. Different people have different ideas on what moderation is. Each of us has a unique value that is unique to us.

Being minimalistic means learning to focus.

Which aspects of your life hold the greatest significance and value? When you focus on the most important and valued items in your daily life, you will realize that although you own many items, only a select few truly add value to your existence. Moderation is the art of knowing what you don't need in your life and when to stop contributing. Then, get rid of stuff and be content with it. The process of minimalism

Being minimalistic isn't a goal in and of itself. It's all about pushing oneself to new limits. It's not hard to identify items and items you don't need, get rid of them, and save only the items that are truly essential to you. Monitoring your requirements daily in moderation.

Time is important in minimalism.

By focusing on the fundamentals, you eliminate complexity from your life. As a result, you get free of false beliefs, anxieties, responsibilities, and tensions. You offer yourself more breathing room when you limit your daily life to only the essentials. You gradually learn to adjust more and use less energy overall. By exercising moderation, you may focus on your most precious resource: time.

What restraint isn't

There are a lot of misunderstandings regarding moderation. Here are a few of them:

The goal of minimalism is to rid yourself of everything. You don't have to give up everything to be minimalist. What you stand to gain by removing items that don't enrich your life should be your first concern.

Life is tougher when you're minimalist: Life isn't harder when you're minimalist. On the contrary, living a minimalist lifestyle makes things easier for you.

Being frugal and minimalism are synonymous: minimalism differs from frugal living in that it encompasses more than just financial savings.

Likewise, the idea that minimalism is solely appropriate for young, single people is untrue.

Minimalism is limited to your possessions: While removing unnecessary items is crucial, minimalism isn't only about that.

How to Become a Minimalist in Chapter Four

In essence, or more accurately, practically speaking, leading a minimalist existence comprises self-improvement, stress reduction, organization, and getting rid of stuff. In its most basic form, minimalism is motivated by these underlying values.

The allure of minimalism lies in its ability to subtly transform your life, leaving behind only the necessities. Eliminating items you value is not, and has never been, the goal of minimalism. It's also not about depriving yourself of experiences that make your life happier and more joyous. Rather, minimalism concentrates on the things in life that are the most significant, certain, and unavoidable. To be honest, if necessary, these developments might take a drastic turn. It implies letting go of really worthless items. Doing this creates more space in your life to enjoy the things that truly bring purpose and worth to it.

It's critical to recognize that living a minimalist lifestyle is a journey rather than a destination. It is a constant process of sorting and eliminating things from our lives, not only material stuff but also the spiritual and emotional facets of existence.

A few actions that can start someone along the path of complete minimalism are as follows:

An assessment of one's life should be conducted to determine priorities.

Assessing one's life in-depth and honestly is essential to being a minimalist. It's the first, and possibly most important, step towards simplifying your life. This step is indeed so crucial that it shouldn't be overlooked. The most crucial aspect of this is to identify what is most valuable and significant to you. Find out which aspects of your life have the most significance, worth, and happiness. You'll be able to set your priorities straight by doing this. It's a lot easier to start the reduction process if you clearly know what is truly important to you. Setting priorities enables one to recognize the advantages of dedicating one's life to only the necessities. Once more, one must comprehend the rationale behind reducing the work. For instance, if there is a place where someone has to stop going, the goal would be defeated, and the explanation would not make much sense if it is not understood and consumed. Then, concentrating on gradually creating more space in your life for your priorities would be simple.

Make a comprehensive self-declaration of the items you own.

Once your priorities have been established, it's time to closely examine your material preparations. Think about what you own and make sure it fits your most pressing needs. Allow it to be a comprehensive and inclusive process. Determine whether the possessions you own enhance your life or if they merely distract you and lead to mental anguish. Even while admitting to oneself can be challenging, in real-time terms, it becomes apparent that most possessions have very little or no value at all. These items may be fancy or amusing "nice-to-haves," but deep down, we know that they don't bring any significance or meaning to our lives. Take the iPhone, for instance, which has 70 applications, only 15 of which are truly valuable. They only squander our time, deplete our energy, or empty our money accounts. Making a list of everything you own that is redundant and no longer valuable to you is a good idea. Getting rid of those things needs to be a gradual and voluntary process.

Make a time audit of your usage.

Being a minimalist means letting go of time-consuming activities and endeavors and cutting back on physical commitments. Thus, the third phase determines how you spend most of your time. Ask yourself if your activities bring value to your life or if they have already added it. De-cluttering will, consequently, give you the advantage of having more time for the things you truly enjoy doing. Determine whether your commitments align with what matters most to your life goals and aspirations. Once you fully grasp how you spend your time, try to cut back on inefficient activities. Once more, begin slowly by addressing the most pressing issues one at a time. Eliminating a bad activity from your life is preferable to trying to combat multiple ones with only half the commitment.

Assess the individuals that received a greater amount of your attention.

Unquestionably, the people you spend most of your time with significantly impact your life. Therefore, it's quite reasonable that you want to interact with encouraging and optimistic people. Simultaneously, minimalism is about recognizing those without toxicity—those who take up your time and energy while providing nothing of value. Start by limiting your time with people who drag you down and hinder you from pursuing your dreams.

Set some boundaries.

You'll discover when you become a minimalist that there are some things and activities you just can't do without. Each of us has regular activities that we are unable to perform without. Depending on who you are or your interests, it might be anything—your phone, computer, internet access, podcasts, etc. The key to these hobbies is to set realistic boundaries and avoid allowing them to interfere with your life. Rather, concentrate on participating in these activities solely within certain times. Set boundaries for whatever you regularly engage in. It will enable you to be more concentrated and productive.

Take out multitasking.

The astounding revelation is that humans are capable of multiplying. Therefore, it is a misconception that one can multitask. One simply shuts down temporarily for the other. When two operations are performed simultaneously, productivity is slowed down. Minimalism disregarding every convention associated with multitasking is detrimental to minimalist ideologies. Single-tasking is the best approach as it enhances focus and thus yields better results.

Establish realistic and minimal goals.

Not every goal can be achieved, and not every goal aligns with an individual's overall health and well-being. To embrace minimalism, one must question one's goals and aspirations and determine whether they align with minimalism—those possessing a decluttering touch. At the extreme, depending on whether all the aspects are considered, one can even reduce it to a single goal.

Be deliberate about it.

The essence of the entire affair is this: minimalism is a retreat from the onslaught of activities and engagements that demand our time and attention. We must take a thoughtful and intentional approach to simplify the things in our lives to approach minimalism fully.

Important Steps to Become a Minimalist in Chapter 2

Now that you know the advantages of leading a minimalist lifestyle and are probably persuaded to do so as soon as possible, it's critical to remember that switching to a minimalist lifestyle is a significant life decision that is neither easy nor quick, like any other. It's more of a journey than a destination, and crucial decisions must be made along the way to ensure that your minimalist lifestyle trip is exceptionally fulfilling.

Don't be shocked if you question how you will ever manage to stick to it after deciding to try living a minimalist lifestyle. You'll be caught between the attraction of a straightforward life and the unease that it might not be easy to get there. In particular, it can be incredibly confusing to figure out how and where to begin minimizing your life because of the massive amount of stuff you've amassed over the years.

One thing to remember is that adopting a minimalist lifestyle is a journey rather than a goal, so it's not something you should do in a couple of days. The likelihood of anyone being able to make the shift in a day or two is exceedingly low, similar to the odds of winning the lottery. However, it is undoubtedly conceivable for a select few people to do so.

You only need to take one or two moves ahead to begin your minimalist journey; simply start with what you now have and can do realistically. As renowned playwright John Heywood once said, "Remember that Rome wasn't built in a day, but they were busy laying bricks by the hour." You must acknowledge that making a significant change, like moving from a life of material excess to minimalism, will require time and consistency. Taking your time and making the shift one or two little steps at a time is acceptable. This way, you can switch to a minimalist lifestyle smoothly and largely anxiety-free.

Let's divide the concepts and actions needed into two categories before discussing the steps you'll need to take to switch to a minimalist lifestyle: recognition and removal. As the name implies, identification procedures entail sorting through the items that are genuinely useful and significant to you and identifying those that aren't. The process of elimination entails taking action to get rid of items you've determined are not necessary for your happiness or quality of life.

Recognize Your Top Priorities

Knowing what matters most to you is the first step in embarking on a minimalist lifestyle—a question only you can truly answer. To accomplish this, you'll need to closely examine your life and determine what makes you feel the happiest and most fulfilled, as well as what causes you the most worry and concern.

More precisely, ask yourself: What aspects of your life can give you the most meaning, fulfillment, happiness, and satisfaction? Once you recognize these items, you can establish rules or standards for what belongs in your possession and what has to go.

Making room for the things that will enable you to live a life of profound joy, fulfillment, and peace will be much easier when you prioritize things or know life. You cannot purge the non-essentials unless you realize how much better your life can be when you make room for the most important things. This is because if you don't realize or appreciate it, you won't be able to let go of everything non-essential due to sentimentality or just plain desire.

TV abstinence is a prime illustration of this. Giving up television is like giving up nourishment for most people. It will be much easier for you to give up TV, though, if one of your priorities is to spend as much meaningful and interactive time as possible with your spouse and children and if you truly understand how watching TV can get in the way of this. You will know your priorities and how TV interferes with them.

The key is that it doesn't have to be anything else. You'll always wonder why you must let go of things unless you understand your priorities and how some things can get in the way of pursuing them. Additionally, your subconscious mind will be able to come up with more excuses to cling to things the more questions you have.

Think Back on Your Items

It's time to take stock of your tangible possessions after determining what matters most. Make a list of everything you own, and after you've done so, consider if each item on your list needs to be in your possession. Think of this approach as a sales pitch or thesis defense; that is, everything on your list of possessions should prove, beyond a shadow of a doubt, why it belongs in your life. Adopt the stance that someone is guilty unless proven innocent or unnecessary unless you can find a good cause for them to continue in your life. By all means, hold onto the material possessions on your list if you can honestly think of ways they will enhance your life and align with your priorities. Expel them if you cannot find a way for them to do so. You should get rid of them even more if you find that they add to your life's chaos, noise, and complexity! Additionally, while purging stuff, start small by selling or donating one or two things at a time.

Chapter 2, Section 8 A Minimalist Lifestyle's Benefits

One method to stop the excess of the world around us is to practice minimalism. It is the opposite of every advertisement we see on the radio and television. Our society thrives on accumulating material goods; we devour consumerism, material belongings, clutter, debt, distractions, and loneliness. What the world appears to lack is any meaningful remaining.

A minimalist lifestyle allows you to get rid of things you don't need so you can concentrate on what you do need.

There is more leeway.

Reducing is the lifestyle of minimalism. A few obvious benefits like reduced stress and cleaning, a more organized household, and more money can be found, but there are also a few profound, life-altering advantages. We rarely realize that we reduce much more than just things when we reduce.

Think about a few advantages of having fewer belongings.

1. Establish a room for what matters.

By clearing out our clutter, we make room for calmness and space. We no longer experience that constriction and can breathe normally. Make space for meaning to enrich our lives rather than stuff.

2. Increased freed

The accumulation of things ties us down, much like an anchor. We always fear losing all of our possessions. If you let it go, you will go through a frenzy unlike anything you have ever gone through: one driven by greed, debt, obsession, and overworking.

3. Put your health and hobbies first.

Spending less time at Home Depot trying to keep up with the Joneses frees up more time to do the things you love and never seem to have time for.

Everyone always claims they don't have enough time, but how many people stop and consider how they are spending their time? You could be spending time with your children, going to the gym, practicing yoga, reading a good book, or taking a trip. Whatever you would love to do, you are stuck shopping for more items at Christmas instead of doing it.

4. A reduced emphasis on material items

Everything we surround ourselves with is a diĕtraction; we are essentially filling a void. Money cannot purchase happiness, but it may purchase comfort. Once the acute discomfort has subsided, that is when our financial obligation should conclude.

The media has surrounded us with false promises of happiness through quantitative measurements. It's no wonder that we battle every day. Refuse those urges. It's a painful path that won't bring you happiness.

5. Greater peace of mind

We produce stress when we cling to material possessions because we are constantly frightened of losing them.

It's that simple: the less you worry about, the more peace of mind you enjoy.

6. More happiness When you're decluttering your life, happiness just seems to come naturally because you gravitate towards the things that matter most. You can see the unfulfilled promises in every chapter; it's as if the real essence of life is being exposed.

You will also experience happiness by becoming more efficient, concentration by refocusing your priorities, and joy by slowing down.

7. The fear of failing

Looking at Buddhist monks, you will see that they are fearless and fearless because they have nothing to lose.

If you're not overcome by the fear of losing everything you own in this world, you can achieve everything you set out to accomplish. Naturally, you must take the necessary actions to cover your head, but you must also understand that you have nothing to fear—except fear itself.

8. Greater confidence

The minimalist lifestyle as a whole encourages self-reliance and individuality. This will boost your self-assurance while you pursue happiness.

Working with Minimalism

You are stuck in your current employment environment. Even while earning a living requires effort, there are still ways to turn this into a means rather than an end. You must find a means to lessen the influence that your current job has on your life if there is no possibility that you will discover another that you enjoy more than it. You may feel overburdened by it or dissatisfied with how coworkers treat you. If you can change employment to something you will like more, take advantage of it.

Step Three: Set priorities for yourself at work.

As an insecure person, you can discover that you have grown reliant on coworkers' praise to feel good about yourself. That's not the best course of action. It suffices to know that you performed well if you do well within the scope of your task; you don't need to tell others. People who seem to need praise will never actually acquire the best jobs because they are too needy; thus, if you can overcome this neediness, you will have a far higher chance of receiving constructive criticism that will help you advance in your career. Here are the things you should try to avoid doing:

Give up multitasking.

Decide what your daily objectives are.

Give tasks to people who are more capable than you. Ensure that your work order is as simple as possible.

Attempting to manage twelve jobs at once is a big source of stress. If you prioritize your tasks and complete each individually, you can finish a dozen tasks more quickly. The optimum time to tackle challenging tasks is first thing in the morning when you get to work because this is when your brainpower is strongest. For example, urgent matters should be at the top of your list. Since you have a deadline, attempt to ask nicely whether someone else can complete any crucial responsibilities you are asked to delegate. Give up attempting to save the day. The person who killed themselves from working too damn hard is hardly the hero. The one who maintains strength and reliability is the hero.

Make sure to allocate a certain amount of time for your daily tasks when you plan them out, and then move on to the next activity. Try not to be a doormat and take on less at once, and people will realize they can rely more on you. You have to realize that being that way isn't helping you. If you look at top management, you'll rarely find a manager so busy that he doesn't have time for management. Less is more when it comes to getting promoted. This entails tackling each task individually and setting a deadline for yourself to complete them. Never try to win someone over. Accept your own speed and try to pick it up over time. Being one-dimensional rather than multitasking can help you boost your speed. Since your minimalistic approach is effective, you'll find that you can handle more responsibility and are trusted with greater authority.

Make sure everything on your desk is organized. Arrange items that are essential to have on your desk. Turn off all distractions. We frequently overindulge in technology using phones, cell phones, social media, and Internet connectivity. Turn it off. It is time to get to work now. When working, schedule yourself to improve your performance within the allotted time. Take breaks when necessary. You can accomplish this more easily with fewer distractions, which you should reduce as much as possible.

You can be experiencing stress if you work from home. You are attempting to balance your personal and professional lives, but frequently you fail. You must discipline yourself to work within fixed hours, like in an office. It's beneficial to have a dedicated workspace where you may isolate yourself from the commotion and noise of your home and avoid feeling bad for neglecting household chores or other obligations. If you eliminate all of these distractions, you'll accomplish more and have more time to spend with your family doing the activities that they expect you to do together.

Even if you work from home, schedule breaks so that you may get up, move about, and have a drink. You need to take breaks. But stay away from social media during work hours, especially during breaks, as it can easily draw you in and consume a lot of time. If you do treat yourself, give it a certain amount of time. Your employment will be more pleasurable and productive if your workspace is less cluttered. It is not difficult to reduce the amount of space in your workstation and keep it tidy and orderly. Every evening after work, you must put in the effort to create an inspiring space and leave it neat and organized for the following day.

Chapter 3: Finances and Simplicity

Since money is essential to our lives, living a minimalist lifestyle does not exclude it. In actuality, managing your finances wisely will assist you in clearing both debt and clutter. You can use the fundamental money ideas of minimalism in your life; this entire chapter is devoted to them.

Adapting Your Financial Attitude

Living with the necessities is central to the minimalist mindset; therefore, removing unnecessary purchases that will just take up space in your home and collect dust is encouraged. When making purchases, minimalists ensure that everything they get is useful or makes them happy.

For instance, you may ask yourself, "Will I be using this pair of shoes at least three times a week?" if you have been considering purchasing a particular pair of shoes for weeks because you adore the style and color. And you can proceed to buy it if your response is in the affirmative.

Some people may view simplicity as opposed to money. This is untrue; in fact, minimalism will enable you to save more money, which you can then allocate to the things most essential to you. Developing a financial minimalism mentality makes you more financially sound.

The Method of Zero-Based Budgeting

Becoming proficient at budgeting is a skill that requires consistent practice. It calls for discipline because you'll be training yourself to resist impulsive purchases and let go of some impulses. However, there is a specific template that you must adhere to to handle your money properly. Although numerous methods are available for managing your finances sensibly, one popular minimalist method is Zero-Based Budgeting.

The Zero-Based Budgeting technique is straightforward: the outcome should be zero if you deduct all your expenses from your revenue. This indicates that you are aware of every expense you make. You are not adhering to the zero-based budget if you manage to pay for all of your bills during the month and find yourself with an additional $100; the same is true if you overspend and end up with a negative amount.

Make a list of your required expenses (food, rent, utilities, insurance, etc.) and subtract them from your total income to implement the Zero-Based budget. Your debts should be settled using the remaining funds. After paying off all of your bills, the money left over should be transferred directly into an emergency fund. This fund will be used when you lose your job, must pay expensive medical bills, or experience other financially stressful crises. Ideally, it should equal three to six months of your monthly salary.

Allocate the remaining portion of your income to retirement plans and investments. Additionally, you might set aside a particular portion for recreation.

Because the envelope system discourages impulsive purchases and overspending (as with credit and debit cards), minimalists typically function on a cash basis. In addition, seeing your money in person and counting it seems far more important than just seeing the numbers printed on paper or a computer screen.

Using envelopes to physically separate your cash for its designated uses is known as the "Envelope System." For example, you've calculated your monthly food and toiletry expenses to about $450. Your bi-monthly paycheck arrives, so you write a cheque for $225, cash it, and put the precise amount in an envelope. Then write "food and toiletries" on this envelope. There is no exception to the rule: you can only use the funds on food and toiletries. For instance, you would walk away from temptations and head home if you happened to walk past a grocery shop without intending to buy anything, even though the bottle of red wine seems appealing. Remember to include your transit costs in the amount of money in the envelope.

Together, the Zero-Based Budget and the Envelope System produce a straightforward but incredibly successful personal finance strategy. For many minimalists, these two are the most prominent budgeting strategies. I hope you'll find them helpful as well.

Living Simply in a Materialistic World

What is the first thought that crosses your mind every morning when you walk outside to your car? Some may wonder if your makeup is smudged or your jewelry is misplaced. You may also be considering whether or not to stop by your neighborhood coffee shop for your favorite cup of coffee because you are running late. Perhaps you're wondering if your suit coat fits properly, if your tie is crooked, or if the way your suit looks will affect your chances of getting your ideal promotion. Perhaps you're looking forward to a shopping weekend with your pals and feel like you need that "retail" therapy to help you unwind after a demanding week.

Nobody pauses to consider the possibility that the additional hour of sleep you could have had instead of obsessing over your cosmetics could have alleviated your fatigue. Nobody considers how their retail therapist will use their credit card and limit their budget for the next month, leaving them more stressed. Nobody ever pauses to consider that your boss is more interested in your performance on the job than in the style of your tie or suit coat.

Now, I'm not saying that leading a minimalist lifestyle entails putting off taking care of your looks, skipping showers to save water for bills, or not giving a damn about how you appear to your boss. What I'm trying to convey, though, is that the tension and fatigue you're experiencing first stem from the emotional impact these things have on your life.

There is simply too much in this world. There are too many jewelry and shoe stores, too many shopping centers, and an excessive number of stores inside those shopping centers. Candle shops line their showroom's square feet with various fragrances, while furniture stores offer far too many options for a growing family to choose from when furnishing their house. Along with this overabundance of products, there is also an excessive number of sellers vying for your business by offering an excessive number of goods. They take advantage of your emotional attachment to objects by persuading you that you might "need" them to establish a fictitious emotional connection. They then spin a tale about how these items will improve your life.

When you get home, you may have spent all the money in your bank account, beach budget, or electricity bill, leaving you furious, anxious, and short on cash.

There is too much of everything in our society, and living a life centeredaround "stuff" is often simpler than living a life centered around "us."

The world is full of activity. In between work and promotions, there are familial responsibilities, friendships you want to maintain if you want to have any sort of social life, and social media accounts beckoning for your presence if you want to stay up to date with modern trends and not fall behind in the world of pop culture. People bring work home with them and stay up until one in the morning, trying to get ahead of the game to advance their position in life.

Given our "instant" culture, it should come as no surprise that men and women between the ages of 25 and 55 most enjoy shopping and making tangible purchases.

It's exciting to think you could enter a store, walk out with something, and hold it in your hands. The concept of "instant" is a welcome diversion from a world where one must work hard over an extended period to receive a meager rise or promotion. Shops and restaurants both profit from customers' desire for rapid pleasure. Your need for rapid access to information, quick uploads, and up-to-date information about your favorite celebrities drives social media.

Because they understand that your life is filled with arduous labor, long hours, and dedication towards an objective that may not even be achievable, they have capitalized on your desire for "instant."

The tale then appears on our phones. A tale about a millionaire businessman who gave up everything to live frugally appears in our instant-access, round-the-clock news feed. It also kills us! Why would someone want to live the same way you do, even if they were leaving behind billions of hard-earned cash? We consider it akin to a slap in the face as if leading a modest life after leading an abundant and wealthy one contradicts your aspiration of working little and never having to worry about money again.

However, a lot of billionaires and millionaires have succeeded. Many millionaire businessmen, including Chuck Feeney, Yu Panglin, Percy Ross, and Jon Pedley, rose to prominence, led extravagant lives, and drank and dined in million-dollar mansions on lush beachfront. However, one day, they decided to give it all up in favor of a more modest way of life.

How To Keep Furniture, Utilities, And Home Décor Minimalist

The next step to simplifying your life is using minimalist techniques for furniture, appliances, décor, and household goods. Let's address each of these components individually.

Interior Design

Almost everyone wants to live in a beautifully adorned home. But this desire frequently leads to abundant ornaments, artifacts, and decorative goods that are either redundant or prohibitively expensive. Accepting minimalism can help you detach yourself from the enormous values you have placed on your possessions and organize your home more effectively.

Deciding to go minimalist with your décor does not imply that you must remove all the vases and ornaments from your coffee table and paint your walls a lifeless color. Rather, it urges you to remove anything put into your home to flaunt your wealth and opulent lifestyle that doesn't belong there.

Analyze the significance of each wall art piece, ornamental piece, decorative item, painting, and vase you have used to embellish your home as you go through every nook, cranny, and room. Determine the meaning behind each item and whether it goes well with your home's general design and aesthetic. Give these goods to someone who might value them if you no longer find the large red vase in your room or the glass bowl on the coffee table useful. Objects that encourage you to improve yourself or that you received as gifts from loved ones should be kept in your home.

Breaking the Cycle of Wants

You will find it tough to break the want cycle on this one because you are mindlessly accustomed to purchasing home décor products and find it difficult to resist the temptation when you see something lovely. However, you must give up this habit to change for the better.

When you see something that catches your eye, try not to snap at it. As an alternative, pause to consider whether you would rather have it in your home in place of something significant, something that truly belongs there. Next, consider whether or not spending a specific sum of money on that item is worthwhile. After you buy the item, that amount will have no utility or function. Additionally, see whether there's a better way to use that money. In conclusion, evaluate if you feel any emotional or inspirational reaction after reading that piece. You should not buy that item if the answer to these questions contradicts your desire.

Furniture and Utilities

Regarding furniture and appliances, you should once more assess the items in your home and remove anything that does not serve a useful purpose. Even if a typical house doesn't contain a lot of furniture, there may be one or two items you have owned for a long time and cannot part with. Discover the cause of your attachment to that particular thing. It's acceptable to keep it if it was a childhood piece of furniture or belonged to your parent or another person you cared about. However, if you're just holding onto it in case you need it for anything else or to add to your furniture collection, it's time to donate it.

Let's go on to the kitchenware and utilities. The golden rule applies: no item should be purchased in multiples. A baking sheet, pot, bowl in each size, and so on are required. Having an abundance of pots and pans that you will never use is a waste of space.

Breaking the Cycle of Wants

To escape the want cycle, you must realize the time, money, and effort that go into maintaining and accumulating items. If you cannot maintain every item you own, it is advisable to donate or throw it away and spend your time on the things that are truly necessary and valuable to you.

Creating A Minimalist Mentality

"Reduce life's complexity by getting rid of unnecessary wants, and life's labours reduce themselves." - EDWIN WAY TEALE

Creating a minimalist mindset is essential before you minimize your house, place of employment, money, or any other area of your life. You will never be able to regulate or alter your beliefs, which leads to consumerism and media bias, until you cultivate a healthy attitude. You must clean your mind if you want to take control of it, quit wanting more, and find meaning in life.

How To Clear Your Thoughts

Here's how to go about doing that.

Pay Attention to the Whys

To inspire yourself to adopt a minimalist lifestyle, list all the reasons you are dissatisfied with your life, then concentrate on those reasons to get inspired to live a truly minimalist existence.

Your motivations may include:

Everything from being tired of debt.

Feeling dissatisfied with your life.

Not pursuing anything worthwhile.

After listing all of these arguments, give them some thought.

Now consider the kind of life you want to lead and write it down. Jot down everything you're grateful for, such as having no stress, a fulfilling career, and no debt. Contrast your desired lifestyle with your existing one. If you practice minimalism, you can readily partake in the latter. You will be inspired to adopt minimalism as soon as you consider how it can help you live your desired lifestyle.

For example, you can pursue minimalism to change the situation where you would like to spend more time with your family but cannot because you need to work longer to satisfy your demand for expensive things. Redefining your requirements and desires and letting go of unneeded wants are two things that minimalism can help you with. As a result, you'll be under less stress and have more time to spend with your family because of the reduced workload.

Use this method to see how every area of your life can be enhanced by simplicity. You'll get additional motivation soon to give up your extravagant lifestyle and embrace minimalism.

Confirm to Yourself the Suggestions Based on Minimalism

It is not enough to simply be driven to live a minimalist lifestyle; you also need to take action, which requires overcoming all the attitudes and beliefs that cause you to desire more. Rewire your brain to be content with less and find fulfillment in the important things in life to achieve this. Using ideas based on affirming simplicity, you can do that.

You provide your subconscious confirmation of something you tell yourself repeatedly. Your subconscious mind begins to embrace things that you often feed it. A notion becomes ingrained in your subconscious and begins influencing your mentality once it is accepted by it. Feed your subconscious mind minimalist-based recommendations to help you become a minimalist. Here's how to go about doing that.

Sit in a quiet place and list all the advantages of minimalism that you linked in the previous chapter.

Affirmations like "I am happy with less and meaningful things in my life," "Less is more and that makes me happy," "I live with things and people that add value to my life and I am happy and peaceful," and other similar ones can now be established.

Make sure the affirmations you use are positive and focused on the present. This means that instead of using words with negative connotations like "don't, not, or never," your affirmation should focus on the here and now with a statement like "I am a minimalist," as opposed to future-focused ideas like "I am going to be a minimalist," which are meant to improve your future rather than your present. Since you want to better your present, create affirmations specific to your current situation.

Recite the affirmation out loud while moving slowly and assuredly. Take your time and concentrate on each syllable as you speak each affirmation. Affirm anything aloud at least 20 times. You will feel calmer at the end of this session and be genuinely inspired to embrace simplicity and put it into practice.

If you practice this practice for ten minutes daily, you will be prepared to embrace minimalism in a few days. When you're ready to commit to minimalism, do it slow so as not to overwhelm yourself and instead engage in consistent minimalism.

Don't implement minimalism in your relationships, finances, place of employment, or home in a single day or week. Instead, dedicate a few days to simplifying your home, health, etc. This allows you adequate time to adjust to any new or different changes you make to your life and ensure you remain with them.

Now, let's explore how you can incorporate minimalism into your house.

Chapter 2: Reducing Disarray

Because it makes you acutely aware of all you have; less is always more. It is visible and unobscured by layers of unnecessary material. Consider whether the furniture in any spare room you may have is necessary or too large for the space. We frequently inherit things and just store them in the spare room since we don't know where else to put them. Then, we get nervous about keeping the room looking nice when we have guests. Since you may utilize this area for other purposes, keeping the room tidy at all times is a much better idea. Nothing prevents you from using the spare room, for instance, if you want to practice yoga or need a quiet place to work on your computer, provided it isn't overflowing with belongings. It also greatly simplifies cleaning.

The plan is to bring a notebook into every room of your home and write down everything that makes your life worthwhile and everything that doesn't. People find it difficult to let go of items. Still, in the end, I've seen so many happy people with the outcomes of decluttering that I know it's a worthwhile task and that life automatically improves when you stop letting your possessions determine their quality. You make your house more spacious. It is simpler to maintain. No items in your possession remind you to spend money or throw money away on useless purchases. What percentage of the clothing in your closet do you wear? Keeping clothes in the hopes of losing weight and fitting into them later comes with a lot of guilt. If you ever reach that point, I promise you won't want your old wardrobe because you'll have established a new persona, and it will be much more likely that you'll go out and buy new clothes. Why fight through the mountains of old clothes, facing that failure every day?

We are all susceptible to being duped by commercials. We buy into the illusion that a magical device will do the laborious tasks we don't want to do when we see it, only to discover later that the numerous responsibilities of using these devices make the effort unworthwhile. Cleaning up the mixer after using it to make cakes, for instance, is more difficult than cleaning up a regular bowl. We thought the deep fat fryer would conceal all the grease, but instead, it harbors it, reminding us how little we've cleaned it every time we open it. An air fryer uses much less space and cooks food without causing tears. You are not depriving yourself of necessities; you are reevaluating your needs to ensure that your home is filled with only items that bring you joy.

You won't have room to conceal your clutter when your wardrobe is overflowing. It is up to you to organize these areas. Why maintain that system if you discover, for instance, that you have a mountain of paperwork organized into boxes? Not only must you handle every piece of paper that enters the house, but you also must store them. The choice is to stop using paper. It means that you force the utilities to store all the paper, but it doesn't mean you can't access your paperwork—you can view previous bills online! You can do the same thing with your bank account.

Even though you may value certain photos and mementos, arrange them all on a table and decide which serve as works of art and which can be digitized so you can have them on memory sticks and access them when needed rather than constantly dust around them.

Your family and your belongings grow together. Examine what is not necessary. Why does that little chair need to take up space in your house when you may have needed it for your son or have been holding onto it for your grandson? Store it in the attic or cellar, wrapping it to prevent damage during storage. Rather than all of this stuff related to past eras, you should have home items relevant to your lifestyle today.

Since technology has advanced, I'm willing to bet that you have bought into the illusion and maybe even have a drawer full of outdated gadgets. This accomplishes nothing for you other than to remind you that your expenditures may have been a bit extravagant. Get rid of anything you don't want. That rainy day will never come, and all of this is piled high in your house as reminders of your past mistakes. You need to realize that giving in to the pressure of social media and television commercials is usually not a better option than giving in to your dreams. You should choose the best phone and stick with it rather than constantly wanting to upgrade.

Anything that is not useful to you should be removed from your home. Being minimalist doesn't mean going without. Making decisions that align with your life is key. It has nothing to do with frugal money saving. It's all about making the most of your lifestyle with the money you have. Purchasing items that become outdated after a week won't truly enrich your life. People make the mistake of believing that all the hype will make them change who they are. Does the most recent iPhone have more features than the previous model? It most likely does, but how significant are the new features in your life? There is little purpose in spending money on something you won't need if they aren't.

Now that you have this mindset, we encourage you to face the reality of what you own in this chapter. It's time to realize the dream and experience the freedom of getting rid of clutter in the upcoming chapter.

The Five Aspects Of Smallness

Authors Joshua Millburn and Ryan Nicodemus outlined the Five Dimensions of Minimalism in their book "Minimalism: Live a Meaningful Life." The dimensions are minimalism's response to the fundamental ideas of happiness as they are now defined by consumerism and conventional boundaries. If you want to be happy instead of just experiencing joyful moments, these are the important things you need to focus on.

After reading this chapter, you will have realized that the following five factors are essential to leading a meaningful life:

- Wellbeing
- Connections

- Emotions
- Expanding
- Input

I'll now talk about each of these and how minimalism is related to it.

Wellbeing

The adage goes, "Health is wealth, not pieces of silver and gold." Undoubtedly, this assertion captures the reality of leading a healthy lifestyle. It is possible to have it all and still not be well. Hold on! Is it even feasible to do that? Our interpersonal interactions could be strained or ruined if we are not well. Our passion could become impossible to follow and develop into something worthwhile and productive if we are not well. Being well prevents us from experiencing self-development, and since we can barely offer ourselves the basic minimum, we are unable to give more to others when we are ill. Without a doubt, then, health is the center of gravity around which the other four aspects of pleasure and a fulfilling life orbit.

When we discuss health, we don't just mean avoiding death—we also mean having a healthy life, which comes down to three main activities: eating, exercising, and sleeping or resting. Eating encompasses not only our meals but also the things we put in our bodies in any way. Food may enter through the skin, nose, or mouth. One needs to be extremely mindful of what they put into their body and abstain from putting anything harmful into them. You could read reputable and accepted diet guidelines and modify your eating patterns to achieve this. Follow the tenet that "you should almost always put only what your body needs in your mouth."

Exercise and the activities we engage in when we want to have fun, rejuvenate, or reenergize our bodies are all included in playing. You don't need to participate in the same sport that someone else does. Exercise caution when deciding what kind of sports you want to play. Select the one that benefits your mind and body, not the one that appears to please everyone.

The health advantages of sleep are immense. Because they know that it boosts productivity, certain oriental cultures allow sleeping during work hours. A person who is under stress is not more productive. He becomes less in it. The brain reorganizes the information gathered during the preceding period of alertness with sleep aid. Furthermore, science has established that a healthy sleep schedule of roughly eight hours is necessary.

Connections

We are the people we spend our time with. Relationships are fundamental to minimalism because they are seen as a means of maintaining and forging new connections. However, partnerships may sometimes be just as destructive as they can be helpful. How? It is a fact that toxic relationships exist, and if they do anything, it is to completely ruin your life. It could be time to break up with your pals if, despite cutting back on excess in your life, you still hang around with people who don't appreciate your decision and actively try to get you to return to your previous wasteful way of living. They are a poison in your relationship because they make you feel inferior to them rather than confident in yourself.

Your interactions will fit into one of three categories: necessary, desired, or unnecessary. You cannot avoid those that are necessary. The bond unites you with your spouse, parents, or kids cannot be severed. Whether you like it or not, these are the folks you need. They are the people you can always count on, no matter what unless things drastically go wrong. At times, your boss at work might also fit into this description. The desirable are people on whom your life does not depend but whose presence gives you happiness, security, and contentment. If your friends are people who enrich your life, then they belong in this group.

It should be noted that people in the first two categories may overlap, and people in the second category may require specific upgrading to the first. Those who gradually wreck your life and those who don't give any value to it make up the last category.

Regarding the former, you should get rid of them because they just take up space in your life and mind. The latter group is even worse; they not only take up your time and worry you out but also actively contribute to your downfall and bring you no benefits. Never be afraid to cut them out.

ardor

A life full of health and happiness would be meaningless without passion. What are your plans for the day? How are you going to change people's lives? How are you going to direct your efforts and desire for personal growth? The solution to this lies in passion. You must have a strong passion for anything. Is it composed? Is it offering services to the community? Is it a competitive sport? There is no reason why you should stop yourself from pursuing your passion, and the whole point of minimalism is to give you adequate time and space—both physical and mental—to concentrate on following and realizing your love.

Expanding

He who stops caring about personal growth is no longer alive. A person who disregards the evolution of their body, soul, and identity is very much dead. He is unaware that he is wallowing in the shadows. He drags himself back and/or down the hill of growth and fulfillment, becoming a liability to humanity. Such a person is not going to find fulfillment and pleasure for themselves. He is more prone to be obsessed with ways to bring others to their knees and, occasionally unknowingly, with ways to impede their progress.

Growing oneself is the only way to advance in life. It is the only thing that provides purpose to our existence. Living a minimalist lifestyle is the first step toward personal growth, but it is not the conclusion of the process. The next dimension is related to the need to move forward in life to bring enjoyment to others and oneself.

Participation

A prior discussion has briefly touched on this final dimension. It moves forward as a result of personal growth. If we cannot demonstrate our beneficial influence on other people's lives, whether through our efforts alone or those of a team, we cannot genuinely say that we are growing or progressing in life. When did you most recently participate in volunteer work in the community? When did you last share some of your good deeds with others? In life, who have you aided? And why is it relevant that you do this action?

Your contribution to the environment, society, and mankind is important because that is where the real peace we all desperately want can be found. The real fulfillment is found there. The peace that comes from remembering how you helped others attain happiness cannot be compared to the sense of fulfillment we get from staring at a picture or painting of our vacation house, our fancy car, or a picture of ourselves on the cover of a fashion magazine.

Chapter 4: Step 2: Get Organized and Declutter Your Life and Space

A room with two tables and around twelve chairs—of which only one is in use, and the other is covered in dust and clutter—looks messier and less appealing than one with a large table and as many chairs as necessary to seat the guests who come over regularly. Eliminating the extra table in that area will increase the room's space and organization and create some mental space and organization. That's the power of minimalism: it makes your life and environment suddenly more manageable by freeing them up.

The next step in being more minimalistic is gradually purging anything in your life that does not help you achieve your goals. Here's how to go about doing it.

Getting Rid of Pointless and Insignificant Items

Examine the different facets of the life you see for yourself. When you get there, how do you want to look? What kind of home are you interested in living in? What kind of work or career do you envision yourself in? At that point, what kind of people do you want around you?

As soon as you have clarity on these issues, use them to simplify your life.

After writing those ideas down in your journal, compare your present situation with every facet of the life you wish to manifest. For example, you should clean and arrange your home to make space if your goal is to live in a large, tidy home where you can cook for your children, but your present home is disorganized. Similarly, you might want to write novels, so you should devote more effort to honing your craft. This calls for you to concentrate on your desire, which you might not be able to accomplish given your cluttered home and your two current employment. You may make more time to write and eventually use it to make a living if you quit one of your two jobs—the one you detest doing—and then sell some of the unnecessary furniture you own.

This exercise's main goal is to help you identify what you want and then make you conscious of all the useless items in your home or activities you engage in that don't advance your objectives. Getting rid of things here implies clearing out your home and getting rid of everything preventing you from reaching your full potential. These are good lifestyle adjustments that you should make but go cautiously.

As previously mentioned, examine the items and pursuits you wish to engage in for as long as it takes, then gradually purge the others from your life.

This is going to be a big change, so start small. Find one item in your home that you no longer use or have a duplicate of, then donate, throw out, or sell it. You can even earn money from the thing you no longer need by listing it for sale on Amazon.com or Ebay.com. That item could be as insignificant as a scarf hanging in your wardrobe or a useless paperweight sitting on your study table. Simply look around you in whatever area or corner of your house, and then give up one useless object from that space.

Jot down your feelings about that little adjustment and hang onto them. Don't discard anything else; instead, return to this task the next day. This time, look closer at the room where you removed the one object and choose any two or three insignificant items. If you recently got rid of something from your kitchen cabinet, go through the entire thing carefully and get rid of two or three things you haven't used in a long time, things you don't need, and things in really bad shape.

Set aside a few days to thoroughly clean the one area or location you've chosen, removing everything but the essentials. After everything is entirely clear, thoroughly clean and organize it, and savor the wonderful sensation you get. Use this emotion as motivation to work on the other rooms in your home and other aspects of your life. Write it down in your journal.

You'll have a much neater, more organized, and appealing home that will improve your quality of life and work in weeks or months.

Next, make sure to tackle organizing your workspace. Examine it thoroughly to determine what you no longer require. Make a note of the tasks you are working on right now, and then go through your computer and look through all the materials, files, documents, and data you need for those projects. Just save what you truly need, and throw away anything you do not need right now. If you need to keep track of previous projects for future reference, collect all the necessary paperwork, arrange it, and put it in a cabinet designated for that purpose or in the storeroom. By doing this, you may avoid mixing up new and old papers, which could lead to an unneeded mess. Junk gets in the way of your crucial work and prevents you from finishing it. Your productivity will, therefore, increase if you maintain a tidy workspace.

After clearing up your home and workstation, purge all unwelcome and pointless pursuits, concepts, and assignments from your life. Work on this assignment using the kind of life you envision as motivation, and use it to identify what you must give up. It's going to be difficult; go slowly.

You will eventually have decluttered your home and life entirely. It doesn't matter if it takes you years to get there; what counts is that you are gradually improving your life.

Chapter 2: Definition of Decluttering

You may easily figure out what decluttering the house entails, but have you ever considered what aids in mental decluttering? This will be a crucial component of your transition to a minimalist lifestyle. The issue is that you have spent so much time in this materialistic world that it will be difficult to adopt a new perspective. That being said, this chapter assists you in clearing your mind and eliminating any cobwebs that could be there. There are a few approaches to this, but you must accept a complete lifestyle shift. Swimming and yoga are two things that will support you during this process. You might be wondering how swimming fits into this. Still, if you practice yoga and meditation, you'll discover that most individuals breathe very shallowly, preventing their bodies from using all their available energy. Swimming is a terrific, low-impact activity that helps you breathe deeply and consistently. Although you may not realize it, swimming also causes your body to release serotonin, increasing your wellbeing.

The baggage you own at home and carry throughout life are identical. It's taking up extra room and adding weight to your load, which is the opposite of what the minimalist lifestyle advocates. While it's acceptable to compartmentalize certain aspects of your life, it's impossible to sufficiently conceal emotional problems. No matter how minimalist you try to be, they will always return. You, therefore, need to address those concerns, and practicing yoga and meditation will support you in doing so.

You should also attempt practicing mindfulness. Instead of prescribing additional medications, which don't seem to be preventing the rise in anxiety-related illnesses, doctors in the UK are utilizing this to assist patients in overcoming their anxiety problems. Stress is encouraged by our way of life, yet mindfulness teaches you to shut off the past, stop thinking about the future, and begin using your senses once more. Letting go of the past is the essence of decluttering, which greatly facilitates your ability to do so.

Your breathing pattern is the first thing you should address. Most people only use the upper portion of their lungs for breathing daily. Still, when you practice breathing techniques, you can do amazing things because the body's sympathetic nervous system is a multipurpose area. When you breathe correctly, your body's neurological system ensures that every oxygen molecule is taken to all the right locations to reduce inflammation and promote overall wellbeing. For this reason, we recommended swimming as a possibly beneficial exercise to attempt to correct your breathing. Although you would not think of it as minimalism, this is. All the tidying up in the world won't make you a minimalist if your mindset isn't right. What constitutes a lifestyle is the way you engage with the environment.

Stopping to smell the roses is necessary. You won't fully embrace minimalism until you have this mindset. Therefore, you must be conscious of what you do to your house and how it helps you. Getting rid of issues and clearing your system of all the ghosts from the past is what decluttering means. All of your thoughts arise because you give them permission to. Learning to meditate teaches you to recognize your thoughts without passing judgment on them. You have the upper hand. That's a pretty effective method of reprogramming the subconscious mind to just let go of things that don't currently apply to your life.

Unnecessary items for your home are less likely to succeed when you are aware of your prior mistakes. Along with appreciating the simplicity of your existence, you can face each day without feeling as though the entire world is pressing down on you—literally or psychologically—due to an excess of possessions.

The upcoming chapter will discuss how you decide what to keep and discard in your life. To restore your sense of wholeness and happiness and regain control over your life, you must let go of your attachment to pointless clutter. You will find tips in the recommendations that will assist you in managing the unnecessary things in your life in a way that is advantageous to you and others.

Handling Money

Your ability to live your desired life may depend on your financial circumstances. Fortunately, it's one area of your life where adopting minimalist principles can have a positive impact. But it's also the most intricate. When managing your finances, what do you even pare down or simplify?

This chapter aims to help you face the reality of your financial condition. You should accept it for what it is rather than brushing it under the rug or downplaying it. Learn how to live a minimalist lifestyle, which can also help you financially.

Shifting Attitudes Regarding Money

Remind yourself of the true purpose of money before obsessing over debt, bills, and other personal finance matters. In essence, money serves as a mechanism for exchanging commodities and services. You can exchange your time and expertise for it. It's also a resource, so you can invest it and make money.

Money is also seen by many as a tool that provides security. After all, it can cover unforeseen medical expenses, repairs, and replacements. On the other hand, some people view money as how they can achieve everything they want. Some become so enamored with the power it bestows upon them that they are prepared to act immorally and illegally.

It's not necessary to go that far. You shouldn't let your need for financial gain rule your life. Don't let your relationships and health suffer for it. Don't put your mental health in danger, either. No matter how strong money gets, it will never be able to purchase happiness.

Contrary to popular belief among materialists and marketers, happiness is an emotion. Purchasing goods and paying for services that may improve your mood is possible. You still can't buy your way to happiness, though. That's something to remember if you are tempted to purchase many items, hoping they will make you happy. You can also recall the instances where you felt bad about making rash purchases.

Expense Advice

You may have taken your home, clothes, and food for granted when you were younger. They seemed to be there all the time. However, you know how stressful it might be to obtain those things now that you are working for yourself. Fortunately, budgeting and minimalist spending can help reduce the anxiety associated with the procedure.

Plan your grocery shopping once or twice monthly to reduce your journeys to markets and convenience stores. Even if ordering groceries online is more convenient, you never know if they will be delivered to your house fresh. In addition, the expenses associated with shipping and online transactions surpass the fuel expenses incurred during in-person shopping. Consider the extra packaging you must throw away once your online-ordered groceries arrive.

Every year, you can get new pants. Regarding clothing, purses, and footwear, adhere to the one-in, one-out rule. This implies that you must discard one item before purchasing a new one. Replace as soon as possible—not simply because anything is brand-new or on sale—and not only because they no longer suit you.

You ought not to purchase it now. Think about it for a few months. If you still enjoy making purchases, do so if you have the money.

Dismissing Consumerism

Reducing consumption appears challenging when advertisements portray all goods and services as necessities. Consequently, materialism grows increasingly widespread. In essence, consumerism is acquiring items in quantities constantly rising above one's necessities. It also includes trying out pointless hobbies and hiring excessive numbers of services.

Many consumers are turning away from some worthless goods and services, in part because of technical improvements and poor pay. That's positive because it makes business owners reconsider their ridiculous offerings. It is also more common for customers to live within their means. Still, some people perceive shortcomings in the circumstances above.

The guilt-tripping of millennials has pushed them to revive sectors they should have crushed. Manufacturing handbags, fabric softeners, beer, cereal, and napkins are among these industries. Additionally, millennials are held responsible for the decline in the appeal of diamonds, motorcycles, and golf. Whether you identify as a millennial or not, you should understand that it is not your role to make sure companies are profitable and able to employ people.

Rather, they must provide something of value.

One of the main forces behind the minimalism trend, which appears to be worldwide, is consumerism. Expect a more difficult time avoiding advertisements and their false messages as long as crafty individuals manage businesses and control marketing.

You can reduce your time watching movies and surfing the web by doing these activities less frequently. Anytime you go through your feed or visit a website, be cautious of anything marked as sponsored. This tag type indicates that a brand has paid for the seemingly natural material.

Additionally, you want to think about unfollowing pages and profiles you are unfamiliar with. In any case, almost all of them are for branding. Even those who appear to be instructive occasionally mention the goods and services of their sponsors without disclosing that they are advertisements. Visit news and educational websites to read the news and learn more.

Steer clear of the deals around the holidays as well. Anticipate inventory sales for numerous brands as well. They also give out freebies and discounts in celebration of milestones. If you don't follow brands on your online accounts, you can avoid many advertisements for these sales. Put in an ad-blocker to further avoid seeing pointless advertisements.

If you must purchase something online, check for trustworthy comparisons and evaluations across two or three sites. When presented with a list of a product's benefits, your reaction should be skepticism rather than astonishment or amazement. The benefit is probably fake or overstated if it looks too wonderful to be true. It is possible to influence reviews as well. There's also a chance the linked sources are faulty. If a scientific study is tagged, verify whether the information provided in the benefits is accurate, selectively chosen, or misrepresented.

It becomes easier to reject consumption if you're having financial difficulties. If you have a serious financial problem, cutting back on your expenditures is your only alternative.

Section 1

Recognize the True Nature of Happiness

Let me tell you, happiness is maybe the most widely accepted concept in American culture, second only to love. You're constantly exposed to the idea of happiness. To be more precise, you hear the word repeatedly. Everyone might agree that happiness is the most important human value. So far, it sounds good, right?

Like how people misuse love, the word is overused to the point that it is meaningless. Do not misunderstand me. It has a meaning, but the confusion stems from the fact that people use it frequently and in many different situations. When someone is trying to sell you something, they often use the word happy or discuss the idea of happiness.

We're all left in this perplexing mist of notions due to this repetitive behavior. Understandably, many individuals are perplexed about what true happiness is in light of the contradicting messages they receive from society. A lot of these signals often contradict one another. They can balance each other out at times.

It's too simple to become lost. Living your life according to a false idea of happiness can be alluring. Ultimately, your attempts to pursue it lead you to pursue something entirely unrelated.

The goal of this book is to solve a problem, but as with any issue-solving endeavor, we must first define some terms to ensure we hit the mark and accomplish our goals. It will be very hard to address if you can't explain a problem clearly. This chapter will set the groundwork for our goals so that we can focus on implementing specific actions to get there.

Contentment Doesn't Come From Your Outside Situations

Understanding the sources of pleasure is the first step towards effectively defining it for yourself. It's far too simple to believe that happiness originates from without. Examples include receiving a present, meeting someone who is highly attractive from the other sex and is interested in you, getting a promotion, and so on. It's simple to assume that you will be happy in any of those circumstances since that's what happiness demands. Outside of you, something occurs.

This is an issue since we obviously have no influence over the outside world. That is not going to occur by itself. Our ability to manage our external circumstances is limited, regardless of our best efforts and available resources.

Since happiness is ultimately what we define as something that has to happen to us, it makes no sense to base our happiness on things we can't control. This is why so many individuals are unable to obtain happiness. Something needs to be in complete control. Even if they might take the lead, it's someone else's call; the circumstances must align, and things must work out a certain way. That's too much to ask for, which is why so many people never find true, profound, long-lasting happiness. It isn't within their power. It's out of their grasp.

The Outcome of Your Internal Expectations and Assumptions is Happiness

Where does happiness originate if it isn't ultimately found outside of ourselves? All OK, go in the other direction. You are the one. Yes, it is correct. Even if you were a rat in a cage, all you would have to deal with was the intense heat, muggy conditions, and insect bites that left your skin raw. It sounds awful, don't you think?

Well, having the correct internal expectations and assumptions might not be that horrible. Read up on Victor Frankl's writings if you need evidence of this. Being a survivor of a concentration camp, he observed that people can alter reality even in the most dire circumstances if they take charge of how they interpret it.

It follows that your external surroundings are irrelevant when applying this idea to real-world situations. Maybe you're in a pit. It's possible that you went several days without eating. Even if many physically uncomfortable things happen around you, you can still feel incredibly joyful if your assumptions and expectations are correct.

Indeed, there are happy individuals in developing nations without running water who endure yearly floods, high crime levels, sickness, and poverty. They give strangers hugs. They are ecstatic to be alive.

Compare this to the sad people who reside in the United States and come from homes with median incomes of over $200,000. What is happening? We are not merely discussing subjective suffering here. We are discussing high suicide rates. How does this fit, then?

The rationale, though, ought to be fairly clear. Your internal presumptions and expectations have an impact on your level of happiness. The favorable tidings? Your presumptions and expectations are up to you. You are not forced to accept them. You don't just get them and must take or leave them. You have the option to select them.

The Republic of the Dominican

I did not visit Mexico. Though I had been there, I was unable to go this time. Although I had Mexico in my sights, fate had other ideas. My friend had tried to convince me several times to relocate to Santo Domingo, Dominican Republic, where he had lived for a few years. He had attempted to persuade me to relocate to California when I was living there, but I had another buddy in Miami, Florida, who had made similar attempts. My acquaintance from Florida told me he could get me a full-time position working for him on Everglades conservation. He offered me $600 a week. I thanked him and turned down his offer with grace. I responded, "No, but I appreciate it!" to my two friends. I desired to be in California.

When I was ready to travel again after recovering from my year in California, my Florida friend had moved on to something else in a different state. My acquaintance remained in Santo Domingo and had no intention of leaving anytime soon. We used to communicate virtually every day online, and one day, he persuaded me to relocate to the Dominican Republic and live close to him. After we spoke about it for hours, he convinced me to make the move. We discussed almost all my worries and objections, and he dispelled them all. I had decided to move to Santo Domingo by the end of the day.

After I made up my mind, the rest of the experience was like when I was getting ready to move to Arizona or California. I wrote a list of everything I would have to do, a small list of things I would need to buy, and a big laundry list of things I would need to get rid of. I intended to take a one-way flight down there and spend at least half a year or more there. I had little money and had no idea where I would live. I would have to travel light, I knew. I had to pare down all I owned until I could fit into two bags. One checked bag and one compact carry-on duffel bag.

A passport was simple to obtain. My auto insurance was simple to cancel. It was also simple to "lend" my mother my car, which they could either keep for me or sell if they needed the money. It was difficult to say goodbye to my friends and family, but they understood I was doing what was right for me and would bring me happiness.

Trying to squeeze everything I owned into two bags was one of the hardest things I've ever done. For me, it was a kind of turning point. It seemed to me like one step towards homelessness. Particularly because I had just $1,800 (USD) in my bank account and was relocating to a different nation, I was slightly alarmed by the modest amount. Still, I soon realized that $1,800 was a significant amount. Sufficient to last me many months till I could secure a source of income. After opening a new checking account at a different bank that provided free international ATM transactions, I transferred almost all of my funds from my previous account to the new one. I had $120 (USD) in cash in my duffle bag and the small amount of money I still had in my previous account. Even though the $120 in cash was ultimately taken, I still managed to move to a nation I had never been to with roughly $2,000. Some thought I was crazy, but I saw it as a wonderful chance to live overseas, visit my friends, and improve my Spanish.

Moving to a developing nation with $2,000, packing up everything you own into two bags, having no employment leads, and having only one good lead on a place to live is about as minimalist as it gets. I should say, one dubious lead on a rental property. I was to rent a room from the building's landlord in the spacious third-floor apartment with three bedrooms. The landlord occasionally resided there, but his permanent abode was a house in the United States. He leased the flat to another guy residing mostly in the United States. I spent roughly fifteen minutes on the phone with the landlord, who informed me that the rent for the next two months would be $425. I agreed but told him I would need to check the location first. I didn't think to inquire about staying for more than two months because it sounded like such a great offer. He said yes after I accepted the arrangement, provided that I first had to meet with him and check the location. After pausing, he asked if I could send the money to him right now. I declined his offer. He stated it was OK when I repeated that I would need to inspect the property first. He informed me that his brother lived on the second floor, would let me into the flat when I arrived, and that his wife would eventually come get the rent. His request to wire money made me uneasy, but I reasoned that I wouldn't have anything to worry about as long as I could rent the place for that amount and make the payment when I got there.

I had clothes in my black suitcase. T-shirts, button-up shirts, shorts, and jeans. I had pens, paper, and envelopes to write and mail letters. I carried five or six thin, short books, including a copy of Of Mice and Men. I only bring it up because the tale's protagonists similarly have simple lives. Socks, pants, and more were in my little black gym bag. It was very hot, so I never wore pants or even half the stuff I brought down there. I also brought toiletries with my passport, checks, and checkbook. $120 cash was stashed away at the bottom of my checkbook box. Six 20 dollars, tucked away and folded into quarters.

I paid $99 for a one-way ticket and left for the Dominican Republic with a black suitcase, gym bag, black dress shoes on my feet, black boots knotted together by the laces and hanging around my neck (I figured I could buy sandals once I was down there), and the clothes on my black. Although my friend who had been living there promised me he would show me around, take me to various locations, and introduce me to some people, I was still a little concerned. I would be OK if I had somewhere to stay for a while.

I was really lucky to get a window seat on the aircraft. My joy at seeing the jungle below as the plane got closer to the ground overcame any trepidation I could have felt. I realized how serious things were as I got out of the airport. I was immediately taken in by the sun, the heat, and the sight of palm trees waving in the light wind. It was one of the most exhilarating experiences I've ever experienced. I can practically smell the salt from the Caribbean Sea as I write about it since I remember it so clearly. After ten minutes or so, my pal arrived to say hello. While waiting for him, I was contacted by two taxi drivers who asked me if I was OK and promised to take me away. As my friend showed up there, he waved for a cab to take us to Santo Domingo, where we caught up and made arrangements. He showed me my new apartment and gave me a tour of the second-floor residence of the landlord's brother. After giving me the keys, the brother gave me a tour of the flat and the roof, to which I would have unrestricted access. After leaving my stuff, my friend and I left again. We headed to supper after he showed me around his flat on foot.

I had an excellent first day in my new nation, and I used the next two weeks to get to know the flat and the surrounding area. Living in Santo Domingo was a minimalist's dream, even though I lived in a lovely three-bedroom flat three houses away from the Caribbean Sea. The landlord, who was also nonexistent, rented out the flat to another nonexistent individual. The landlord rented out the other two bedrooms whenever possible since the second guy was never around. I claimed one bedroom, while a Norwegian guy who was never there claimed the other.

The flat lacked food despite having a full-sized refrigerator and a fully equipped kitchen. The next morning, I had breakfast outside. You don't eat out for breakfast in this utopia for minimalists, within a few blocks of wherever you walk on the street. I did precisely that. On my first day, I had three bananas and a plate of sliced papaya, mango, and pineapple (known as "lechoza" in the Dominican Republic). Greetings from the Caribbean! Each banana costs five pesos or around eight pesos for a dollar. I would soon discover that all the fruits that grow there are cheap, including the mixed fruit. I discovered that my apartment's roof was almost an orchard in and of itself. There was a massive mango tree growing next to the building, and twice a year, the tree would yield more mangos than the occupants of the building could consume. Regretfully, neither mango season was I there. It was not to be, but I would have loved a tummy full of fresh mangos I had selected.

Media: For this discussion, "media" refers to books, CDs, DVDs, and any comparable media collection. Think about the amount of room you have set up for this material. Some people have cabinets, drawers, and collections of these kinds of media. If things are important to you, value them as much as you like. In the unlikely event that you enjoy the content in the media but detest the amount of space they take up, fear not! You may continue using your drug while saving money on space in a few different ways.

Nowadays, most media—though maybe not all—can be accessed online in one form or another. It may be through a record label with which you currently have a record, or it could be through a label that makes it incredibly easy to create one. These days, when you purchase a DVD, you frequently find a code inside the case that allows you to view an advanced copy of the movie. Why spend the (usually) extra money to purchase the DVD in a store when you can locate the content carefully for less money? Perhaps renting a movie is a more feasible financial option for you. In any case, how many of your films do you view at different times?

Magazines and papers may be incorporated into other media. It's not unusual to see enormous piles of magazines or papers in some households. If you identify with this and want to rid yourself of the mess, you might want to save the most recent version of each item. Maybe you could watch something similar online, or maybe you could live without it entirely? Perhaps you watch the media and repurpose it once its contents are finished.

Online scheduling makes your media accessible from anywhere you go to manage the capacity for you. There's also usually less possibility of damaging or losing the substance, no extra shelf, and dust. The circles won't ever scratch, the computerized pages won't tear, etc. Think about using an optional method to consume your media.

Decorations:

When discussing stylistic layout, we will consider any enhancing elements besides images, outlines, or other interior décor. A lot of people value the beautiful decorations in their living room. In the unlikely event that this worries you, continue to enjoy the joy that such a style affords you. Thinking about your options if you feel that being aware of these things is a chore.

Several improvements hardly need any help at all. Consider maintaining a certain amount of items improved. Replace a more seasoned item if you acquire or walk over another one that you might want to use. The old item is always available, or you can give it to someone else who might find value in it. Authentic or fake plants, souvenirs from a memorable period of your life, great paintings, and so on are items you might find useful to have around. You can easily arrange items across your living area and class them as décor.

The same applies to the images that you have throughout your house. Although showing off your family is undoubtedly fantastic, it can be difficult if you have too many or non-set photos of them. Again, consider the most prestigious people as you show off your pictures. Make thoughtful choices because these will have a big impact on your reality.

In brief:

Your lounge is a vital area where you and your loved ones may get together. This area will reveal a lot about your life experiences based on what it looks like. More room can mean more room for your family to walk about and enjoy one another's company. Choosing the items that are most important to you will help you create the lifestyle that you most desire.

Kitchen Minimalism

For many individuals, the kitchen is an essential component of their house. The food is set out here to give us the nourishment we need to start our days. This area is essential in many homes since large appliances can occupy precious square footage. No matter the size of your kitchen, you can create a workspace you love by making the most of every square inch of the floor, pantry, and counter.

Appliances:

For your kitchen to be functional, selecting the appliances that are best for you is essential. In addition to taking up space, choosing items with high energy consumption might result in expensive electricity costs. Choose ovens and stoves that suit your needs in size and features. Determine whether you need a dishwasher and whether you have the space for one. Determine which additional kitchen tools are essential to you. These could include microwaves, toasters, toaster ovens, and other appliances. Release yourself from the excess if you think you have a device that three people created.

In the unlikely event that any of the appliances in your kitchen are no longer valued or necessary, make this decision. Does your coffee maker just take up space in your home? Was that juicer looking wise at that point? It's acceptable to realize that these things are currently useless and to move on from them. Furthermore, getting coffee outside the house is usually just as entertaining as cleaning the machine.